The Joy of Piano Entertainment

Compiled and arranged by Denes Agay

FOREWORD

This volume, as its title implies, is designed to be a handbook of musical diversion and conviviality. Pianists—young and adult, amateur and expert—will find here an ample and appealing repertory of melodic pieces for relaxed, easy playing, as well as for furnishing an always welcome background for singing, dancing or just pleasant listening. The contents, ranging from Baroque to Jazz, from Mozart to Scott Joplin, present a wide and colorful variety of vocal and instrumental favorites to suit many moods, tastes and occasions. The selection of materials and arrangements are the work of Denes Agay and reflect his widely respected taste, craftsmanship and epicurean love of all kinds of good music. The *Joy of Piano Entertainment* will provide many moments of musical pleasure for players and listeners alike.

The Publishers

Cover illustration by Melanie Arwin

e d c b

International Standard Book Number: 0-8256-8020-4
Library of Congress Catalog Card Number: 77-83768

Distributed throughout the world by Music Sales Corporation:

33 West 60th Street, New York 10023
78 Newman Street, London W1P 3LA
4-26-22 Jingumae, Shibuya-ku, Tokyo 150
27 Clarendon Street, Artarmon, Sydney NSW
Kölner Strasse 199, 5000 Cologne 90

Contents

Sleepers Awake

Theme from *Cantata No. 40*

Johann Sebastian Bach

Baroque Fanfare

Jean Joseph Mouret

Jesu, Joy Of Man's Desiring

Johann Sebastian Bach

Theme from Piano Concerto
K. 467

Wolfgang Amadeus Mozart

Themes from "Rustic Wedding" Symphony
1. In the Garden

Karl Goldmark

2. Bridal Song

Intermezzo

Romance

from the opera *The Pearl Fishers*

Georges Bizet

España

Emil Waldteufel

Swedish Polka

Theme from *Swedish Rhapsody*

Hugo Alfvén

Serenata
Rimpianto

Enrico Toselli

Hungarian March

from *The Damnation of Faust**

Hector Berlioz

*Traditional melody, known as "Rakoczy March", named after a 17th century Hungarian revolutionary leader.

D.C. al Fine

Echoes of Vienna

"Tales from the Vienna Woods"- Johann Strauss

"My Life Is Love and Pleasure"- Joseph Strauss

"Radetzky March"- Johann Strauss, Sr.

Nola

Felix Arndt

Whistling Rufus

Lively cake-walk tempo

Kerry Mills

Trio

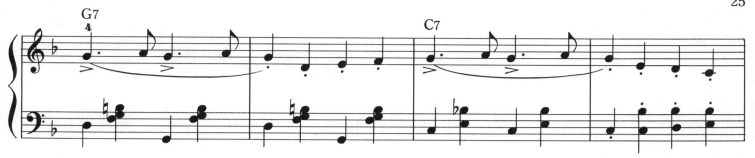

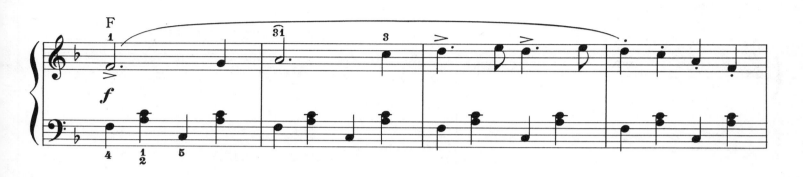

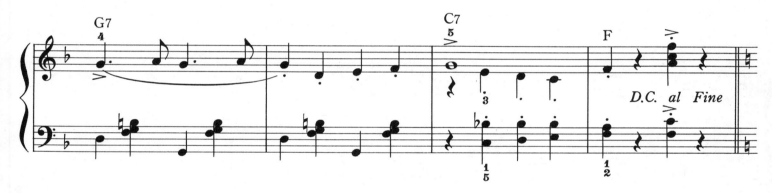

Hava Nagila

Bright tempo (Hora)

Israeli Folk Dance

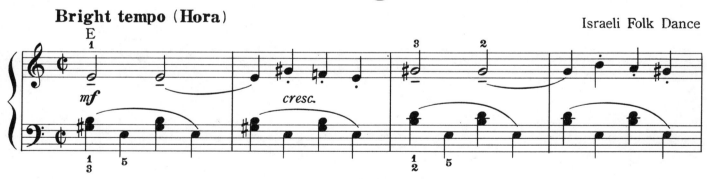

Pomp and Circumstance

Edward Elgar

Joplin Gems
Themes from *The Entertainer, Solace, Original Rags*

Scott Joplin

Very slow "Solace" (A Mexican Serenade)

Polka Italiana

"Oh, Marie"-"Funiculi, Funicula"

Arranged by
Gerald Martin

E. di Capua
L. Denza

Very lively

March of the Toys

from *Babes in Toyland*

Victor Herbert

Little Rhapsody on Gypsy Tunes

Moderato; freely

Gerald Martin

"The Sleeping Beauty" Waltz

Peter I. Tchaikovsky

Lively waltz tempo

*Lower octaves are optional

Music Box Rag

Denes Agay

The Toy Trumpet

Raymond Scott

Jazzy Little Brown Jug

Gerald Martin

By The Sleepy Lagoon

Waltz Serenade

Eric Coates

48

"Easy Rider" Boogie

Arranged by
Gerald Martin

The Washington Post

John Philip Sousa

Lively march tempo

Hesitation Waltz

from the ballet *The Red Poppy*

Reinhold Glière

Slow waltz tempo

Let's All Be Friends Again

Moderately, with a happy beat

Russian Gypsy Song

Let's all be friends a-gain,___ Let's all have fun a-gain,___

___ Come on and sing, it's here where you be - long.___ Show us a

smil - ing face,___ The world's a fin - er place,___ if we are friends and

join in hap - py song.___ Let's all be song.___

When You Were Sweet Sixteen

James Thornton

Meet Me In St. Louis, Louis

Andrew B. Sterling

Kerry Mills

I Am The Very Model

from *The Pirates of Penzance*

William S. Gilbert

Arthur Sullivan

A Wand'ring Minstrel

from *The Mikado*

William S. Gilbert

Arthur Sullivan

I Have a Song

from *The Yeomen of the Guard*

William S. Gilbert

Arthur Sullivan

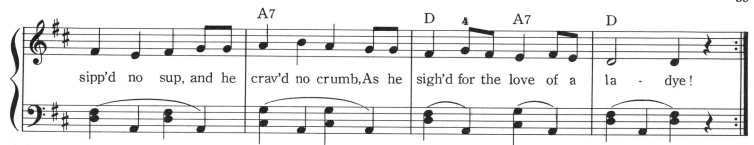

sipp'd no sup, and he crav'd no crumb, As he sigh'd for the love of a la - dye!

Just A-Wearyin' For You

Frank Stanton

Carrie Jacobs Bond

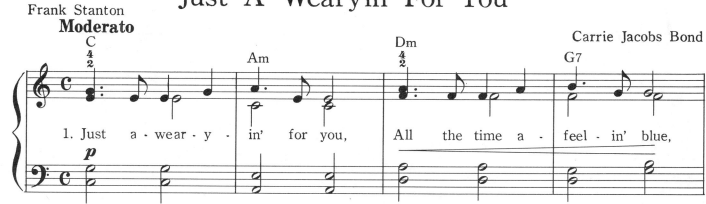

1. Just a - wear - y - in' for you, All the time a - feel - in' blue,

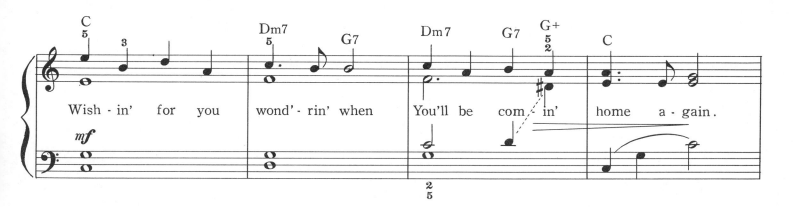

Wish - in' for you wond' - rin' when You'll be com - in' home a - gain.

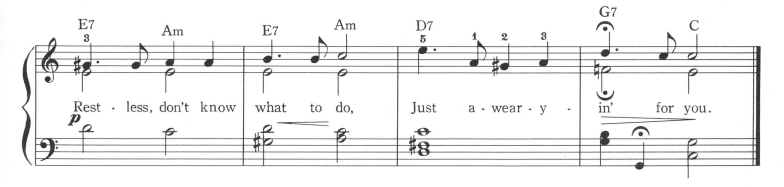

Rest - less, don't know what to do, Just a - wear - y - in' for you.

2. Mornin' comes, the birds awake,
Used to sing so for your sake,
But there's sadness in the notes
That come trillin' from their throats.
Seem to feel your absence, too,
Just a-wearyin' for you.

3. Evenin' comes, I miss you more
When the dark gloom's round the door,
Seems just like you orter be
There to open it for me.
Latch goes tinklin', thrills me through,
Sets me wearyin' for you.

This Old Man

Play Tune

Rather lively

*This old man, he played "one," He played "nick-nack" on my drum,

"Nick-nack pad-dy whack, give my dog a bone," This old man came roll-ing home.

*Make up your own rhymes for the successive numbers, "two" to "ten."

Tell Me Why

Traditional Song

Tenderly

Tell me why the stars do shine, Tell me

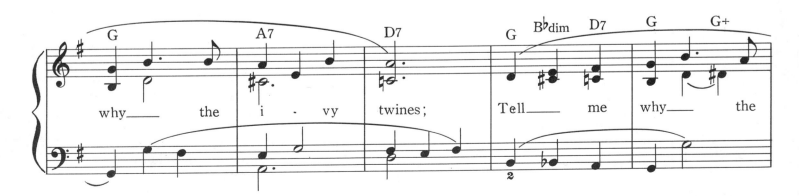

why the i-vy twines; Tell me why the

skies are blue, And I will tell you why I____ love you.

Michael Finnigan

Play Tune

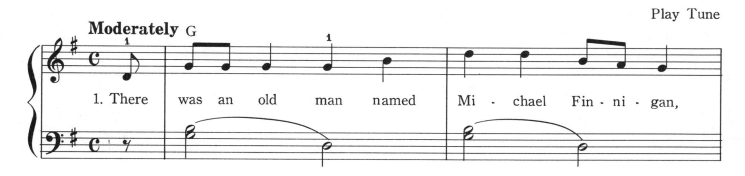

Moderately

1. There was an old man named Mi - chael Fin - ni - gan,

He grew whisk - ers on his chin - i - gin, The wind came up and

blew them in a - g'in, Poor old Mi - chael Fin - ni - gan, be - gin a - g'in.

2. There was an old man named Michael Finnigan
He got drunk through drinking ginnigan,
That's how he wasted all his tinnigin,
Poor old Michael Finnigan, begin ag'in.

3. There was an old man named Michael Finnigan
He grew fat and then grew thin ag'in,
Then he died and had to begin ag'in,
Poor old Michael, please don't begin ag'in.

The Animal Fair

Rise And Shine

Play Tune
(Based on a Spiritual)

Moderately lively

1. Rise ___ and shine ___ and give God the glo - ry, glo - ry,

Rise ___ and shine ___ and give God the glo - ry, glo - ry,

Rise and shine and give God the glo - ry, glo - ry, Chil - dren

of the Lord. ___

Lord. ___

2. God said to Noah, there will be floody, floody (twice)
   Get your children out of the muddy, muddy,
   Children of the Lord.

3. Noah, he built him, he built him an arky, arky, (twice)
   Made it out of hickory barky, barky,
   Children of the Lord.

4. It rained and rained for fo-orty days-y, days-y, (twice)
   Drove those couns'lors nearly crazy, crazy,
   Children of the Lord.

5. The sun came out and dried up the landy, landy (twice)
   Everyone felt fine and dandy, dandy,
   Children of the Lord.

The Big Rock Candy Mountain

Folk Song

64

Bill Groggin's Goat

Moderately

Traditional

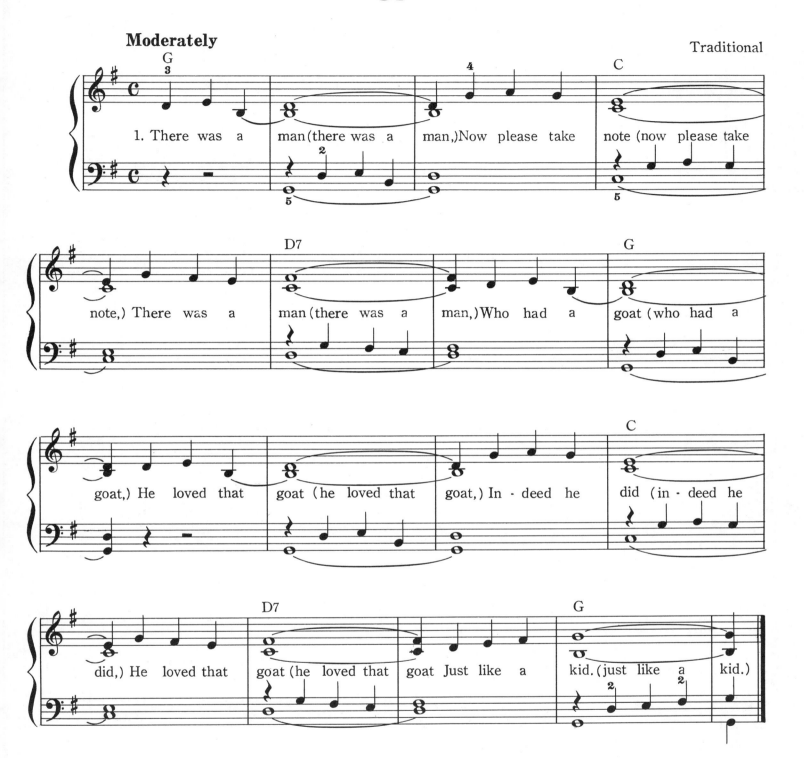

2. One day the goat
   Felt frisk and fine,
   Ate three red shirts
   Right off the line.
   The man he grabbed
   Him by the back,
   And tied him to
   A railroad track.

3. Now when that train
   Hove into sight,
   That goat grew pale,
   And green with fright.
   He heaved a sigh,
   As if in pain,
   Coughed up the shirts,
   And flagged the train.

Morning Has Broken

Gaelic Melody

1. Morn-ing has bro - ken Like the first morn - ing;
Black - bird has spo - ken Like the first bird.
Praise for the sing - ing! Praise for the morn - ing!
Praise for them spring - ing Fresh from the Word.

2. Sweet the rain's new fall
   Sunlit from heaven,
   Like the first dew fall
   On the first grass.
   Praise for the sweetness
   Of the wet garden,
   Sprung in completeness
   Where his feet pass.

3. Mine is the sunlight,
   Mine is the morning,
   Born of the one light
   Eden saw play.
   Praise with elation,
   Praise every morning,
   God's recreation
   Of the new day!

Amazing Grace

Folk Hymn

1. A - maz - ing grace, how sweet the sound, That saved a

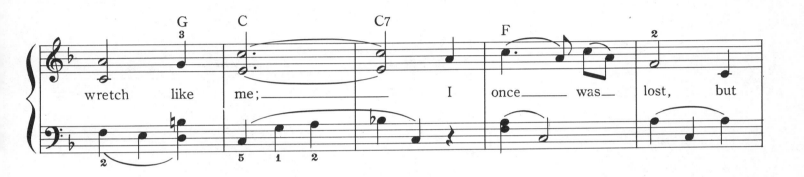

wretch like me; I once was lost, but

now am found, Was blind but now I see.

2. 'Twas grace that taught my heart to fear,
   And grace my fears relieved;
   How precious did that grace appear
   The hour I first believed.

3. Thro' many dangers toils and snares,
   I have already come;
   'Tis grace that bro't me safe thus far,
   And grace will lead me home.

4. How sweet the name of Jesus sounds
   In a believer's ear;
   It sooths his sorrows, heals his wounds,
   And drives away his fear.

5. Must Jesus bear the cross alone
   And all the world go free?
   No, there's a cross for ev'ry one
   And there's a cross for me.

Strolling At Loch Lomond

Gerald Martin

Leisurly, with a solid beat

Variations on "Happy Birthday"

in various styles from Bach to Boogie

by Denes Agay

Theme

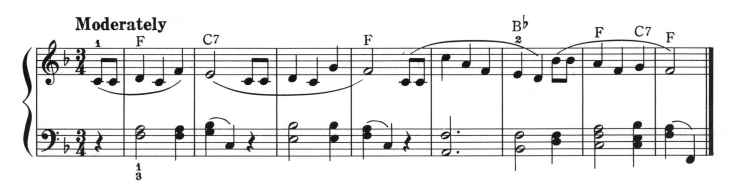

Variations on "Happy Birthday"

from Bach to Boogie

Denes Agay

Variations on "Happy Birthday"

Allegretto cantabile (... Mozart)

Variations on "Happy Birthday"

Variation on "Happy Birthday"

Allegretto (... Schubert)

Andante con moto (...Chopin)

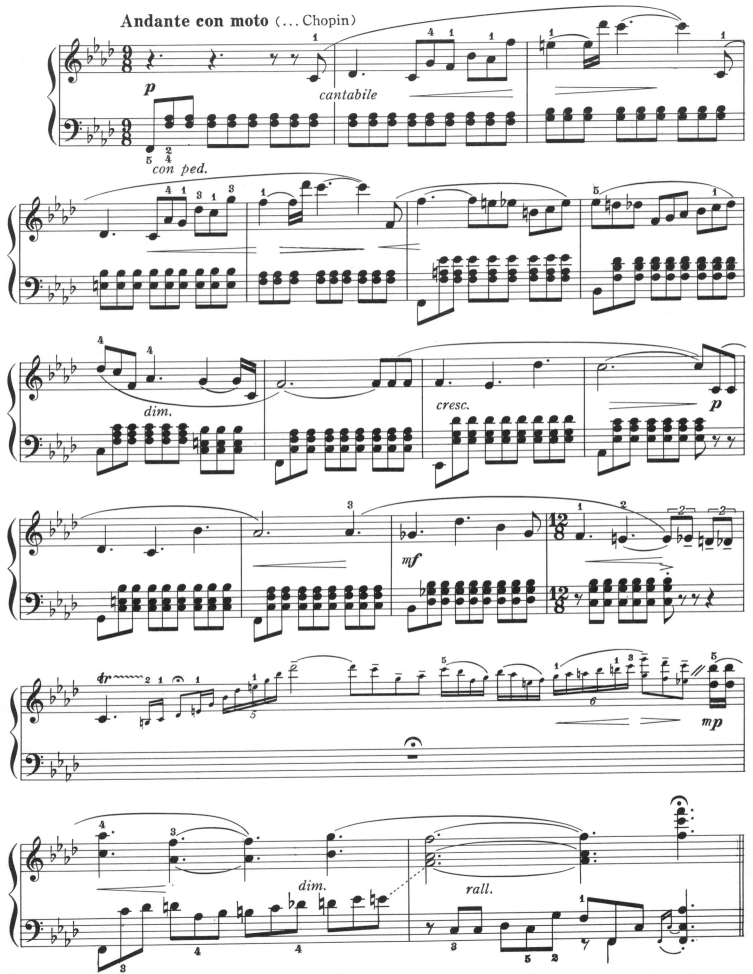

Variations on "Happy Birthday"

Variations on "Happy Birthday"

Moderately lively waltz (... Johann Strauss)

Variations on "Happy Birthday"

D.C. al Fine

Lively March (... John Philip Sousa)

D.S.

Variations on "Happy Birthday"

Con moto, delicato (... Debussy)

Variations on "Happy Birthday"

Slow, steady beat (...Ballad à la Gershwin)

Variations on "Happy Birthday"

Fast, driving beat (... Boogie Finale)